Hamlyn **DOG BREED** Handbooks

Yorkshire Terriers

Angela Sayer & Edward Bunting

HAMLYN

First published in 1988
by The Hamlyn Publishing Group Limited,
a Division of The Octopus Publishing Group plc,
Michelin House, 81 Fulham Road,
London SW3 6RB.

ISBN 0 600 55793 6

Printed by Mandarin Offset in Hong Kong

Contents

Introduction

The Yorkshire Terrier is the smallest breed of dog that is at all commonly seen. For 25 years this toy breed, weighing less than the average cat, has enjoyed a position of star popularity throughout the English-speaking world as well as in Western Europe and Japan.

This development can be explained largely by the unique character of the Yorkie, for there is really no other dog quite like it. Friskiness, humour, adaptability, friendliness and trainability are packed into so tiny a frame that it seems a miracle. And the Yorkshire Terrier is so fascinating to watch because it seems to pay no heed whatsoever to the difference in size between it and other dogs.

A Yorkie seems to think it can do everything that a 'normal' sized dog can do, if not better, and the look in its face with its dark, twinkling eyes, seems to say, 'Forget about my long, silky coat and the red ribbon on my topknot – I'm a terrier and I'm fighting fit!'

The coat is wonderfully silky and long. On a prize specimen, and many others besides, it reaches to the ground and trails a little way behind as the dog walks. Yorkshire Terriers have two colours: blue (which means dilute black) ranging from battleship grey through steel blue to near-black; and tan, appearing on the face and feet, shading from a rich tan at the roots to light tan at the tips. And the coat sparkles and shimmers as it catches the light.

Owners find it well worth the trouble to give this coat maximum attention every day. After months of patient grooming and shampooing the result is breathtaking. Owners of dogs that are not destined for a show career often keep the hair cropped fairly close, saving themselves a lot of work and allowing the dog greater freedom of action in its everyday life.

Yorkshire Terriers are born black and their coats lighten as they grow

An inseparable part of the breed's character and 'personality' is the story of how it came into being. Only five human generations ago the Yorkshire Terrier was just being invented and the qualities of the breed still had to be fixed. The first truly famous champion was Huddersfield Ben, who was born in 1865. The history is, in a nutshell, of a pocket-sized ratting dog, kept by working men such as miners and factory employees in Yorkshire, that was found to match the needs of fashionable society for a glamorous toy dog. Thus the Yorkshire Terrier replaced the pug dogs that are seen in portraits of aristocratic ladies of even earlier times.

The matchless sheen of a champion's coat

Yorkshire Terriers have many advantages for the owner who has more of an indoor lifestyle or lives in a town. Being so small, they can live hapilly with less exercise than a larger pet, and there is room for them if you live in a flat without much extra space. They do not moult, which is both unusual and very convenient from the point of view of maintaining carpets and furniture. They will never miss the sound of someone approaching, and the alarm they raise is shrill and audible, while an intruder might least expect trouble from so small a dog – so they are tiny but very efficient guard dogs.

On the other hand they will gladly take to a more outdoor life: they simply love to play hunting games along hedges and country lanes, and a Yorkie weighing 2.4 kg (5 lb) can easily run 8 km (5 miles) every day once it is used to it! They can be trained to relate very well with new aquaintances (introduced by their owner) and are trusting and intelligent companions. A well-managed Yorkie will always be affectionate and obedient.

Breed standard

How does the judge know what to look for? The Kennel Club, in Britain, is the organization that sets the standard for each breed, and this is always done in collaboration with the main club or clubs connected with the breed. The last revision of the standards was published in the summer of 1987.

The information we present here is a simplified version of the official standard for the Yorkshire Terrier, which goes into considerable detail and would fill about four pages. The standard is often expressed in words or phrases that form a kind of jargon to owners in the breed; and it is often up to an individual judge to decide how the wording of the standard should be interpreted.

Right and wrong ear conformation

Correct
Small, V-shaped ears, carried erect

Incorrect
Floppy ears

Incorrect
Semi-erect ears

Yorkshire Terrier

Ears   Small, v-shaped and covered with short tan hair; carried erect or semi-erect

Eyes   Dark, intelligent; medium size, not bulging; eye rims dark

Head   Relatively small and flat, with a rather short muzzle and perfect black nose. Level jaw, scissor bite

Colour   Steel blue from back of head (occiput) to root of tail; rich tan on chest. Tan hairs are darker at roots, paler at tips

Faults   Prominent eyes; curly hair; silver-blue coat; tan coat spotted; blue coat brindled

Height   No standard given for UK

Weight   Up to 3.2 kg (7 lb)

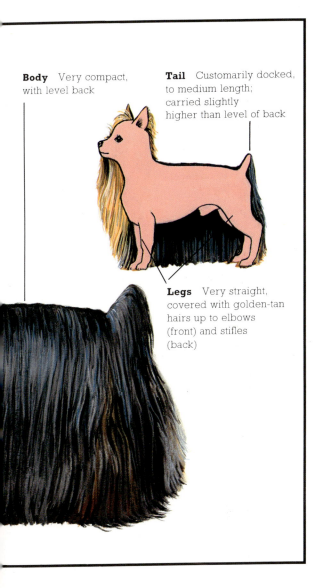

Body Very compact, with level back

Tail Customarily docked, to medium length; carried slightly higher than level of back

Legs Very straight, covered with golden-tan hairs up to elbows (front) and stifles (back)

Incorrect tail carriage

Correct tail carriage
Slightly higher
than the line
of the back

Roach back is an
incorrect curvature
of the spine

Right and wrong body conformation

So the only way to explain the standard really clearly would be to print it in full, and follow it with a commentary from a well-known judge, which may even be twice as long as the standard itself.

Judging is an art, and ultimately a matter of personal taste, based on long experience of showing and breeding. The written standard may be the 'law' but the work of the judge is to interpret it, case by case.

Registering and showing

When pedigree puppies are born, it is normal to register them with the Kennel Club. It is best, and cheapest, if the breeder registers them, but you can do so if you have just bought a puppy and find it is not registered – provided the breeder has registered the litter initially.

The breeder normally fills in a Kennel Club registration form which can either be used simply for an initial registration of the litter, or for the individual registration of each puppy.

Registration is crucially important if you ever want to take up showing or breeding for show, for any dogs that lack registration papers will never be able to attend any show of any importance, nor will their offspring be able to attend either.

Ownership is shown by a transfer form (on the reverse of the green-and-white Kennel Club registration certificate) made out in the name of the purchaser of the puppy, and signed by the breeder.

A pedigree dog has a kennel name, given to it by the breeder, which normally consists of the affix and the dog's individual name. The affix can be either a prefix (first name) or a suffix (last name or phrase) and serves to identify the dog as coming from the kennels where it was born.

Once a dog is registered, its kennel name cannot be changed and no other dog can be given the same name within less than 10 years. The dog's everyday or 'calling' name may be different from the kennel name and is the name to which the dog responds and which is used to give commands.

Types of show

Exemption show For this and this type only, dogs are exempt from the need to be registered. It is the most informal of all kinds, and is not held by a breed club: charities, agricultural shows and village fetes are the usual sponsors.

Sanction show This is an informal members-only show held by a local canine society or a breed club. For example, the Barking Canine Club (it really does exist!) held a sanction show on November 16th, 1987, at Ilford in Essex.

Limited show Also organized by a local society, but at a more formal level. Confined to members of the society.

An exemption show is the least formal

The show box – used for transit, and as a stand for exhibiting

Open show Open to any dog that is registered; it is held by a local canine society or by a breed club. When a canine society catering for a variety of breeds or all breeds holds an open show, all these breeds will be admitted. For example, the South Western Toy Dog Club's open show in October 1987, in Bath, catered for all the recognized toy breeds. At the Yorkshire Terrier Club's open show on the other hand, held in September 1987 at Bounds Green, only Yorkies were shown.

Championship show This is an open show, except that the standard is even higher and the proceedings are much more formal. The Kennel Club offers Challenge Certificates for the best of sex. If a dog wins three of these it is entitled to the prefix 'Champion' to its name. The Yorkshire Terrier Club's championship show was held on December 5th, 1987.

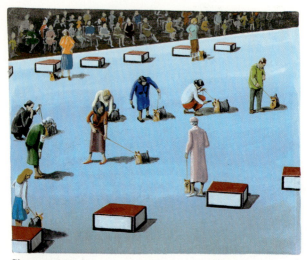

Show dogs must stand patiently while the judge examines them

In addition there are the group and general championship shows such as Cruft's and the regional shows held around the United Kingdom, such as the Manchester Dog Show or the United Kingdom Toydog Society Show. These are the really large events capturing the news media, but are of less concern to the owner who is just beginning as a breeder and showgoer.

Breed clubs
The Yorkshire Terrier Club (founded 1898)
Mrs P Osborne, 19 Avebury Avenue, Ramsgate, Kent. Tel. 0843 597683
Cheshire and North Wales Yorkshire Terrier Society Mrs P M Grunnill, 16 Brook Lane, Chester CH2 2AP. Tel. Chester 382612.
Eastern Counties Yorkshire Terrier Club
Mrs M Millward, Sanbar, Main Road, South Reston, Louth, Lincs. Tel. 0521 50437.

Lincoln and Humberside Yorkshire Terrier Club Mr B F Shirley, Windmill Bungalow, Bucknall, Lincs. Tel. 052685 216.

Midland Yorkshire Terrier Club Mrs K Naylor, Holly Cottage, 356 Lichfield Road, Burntwood, Walsall, Staffs. Tel. Burntwood 71082

Northern Counties Yorkshire Terrier Club Mr A Blamires, 482 Bradford Road, Brighouse, W. Yorkshire HD6 4ED. Tel. 0484 712678

South Western Yorkshire Terrier Club Mrs I M Millard, 6 St Andrews Road, Backwell, Bristol BS19 3DL. Tel. Flax Bourton 3689

Ulster Yorkshire Terrier Club Miss M Callen, 19 Woodvale Road, Belfast BT13 3BN. Tel. Belfast 744853

Yorkshire Terrier Club of Scotland Mrs M Rillie, 129 St Quivox Road, Prestwick, Ayrshire. Tel 0292 76072

Yorkshire Terrier Club of South Wales Mr M D Owens, 29 Rhydyffynnon, Pontyates, Llanelli, Dyfed. Tel 0269 860543

Other useful addresses

United Kingdom Toydog Society New Bingley Hall, Stafford; Mrs D Dearn, 33 Storforth Lane, Hasland, Chesterfield, Derbyshire.

The Kennel Club 1–5 Clarges Street, Piccadilly, London W1Y 8AB

Ladies' Kennel Association Miss M S Churchill, Yew Tree Cottage, Horsley, Nailsworth, Gloucestershire.

Royal Society for the Prevention of Cruelty to Animals (RSPCA), The Causeway, Horsham, West Sussex RH12 1HQ.

Our Dogs magazine, 5 Oxford Road, Station Approach, Manchester M60 1SX.

Dog World magazine, 9 Tufton Street, Ashford, Kent TN23 1QN.

Choosing
the right puppy

At birth, a Yorkshire Terrier puppy weighs only a few ounces, perhaps typically 100 g (4 oz). The adult weight varies between extremes of as little as 0.45 kg (1 lb) and as much as 4 kg (8¾ lb), with the occasional enormous one weighing even more.

By the time a puppy is of saleable age at 2–3 months, its weight could be 0.25 kg (½ lb) or as much as 2 kg (4½ lb). Not that many breeders would allow a half-pound puppy to leave home! This variation in weight is not matched by variety in colour, at first: for all the puppies are born black and tan. But there are many other variables to look at, so how should you choose which is the right puppy for you?

Make sure that you start at the right place. The Kennel Club will give you the address of breeders in your area, or with the address of the Secretary of the breed club most relevant for your area. Find a breeder who has or is about to have puppies for sale and make an appointment to visit the kennels.

Perhaps you already know what sort of a life your Yorkshire Terrier will live. If you simply want a pet, and not a show dog, you probably know it. Or are you likely to take an interest in showing later on? You might wish to keep your options open and acquire a bitch who will be a good pet but, should you have the time and inclination in another year or two, will serve as the foundation bitch for your own breeding line.

Be prepared to discuss these plans fully and openly with the breeder. It is no good asking for a pet dog and secretly hoping to come home with a prizewinner 'on the cheap'; puppies that are sold as pets are ones that have some feature such as markings or the angle of the

Once immunized, puppies may play out of doors

ears that would bar them from a show career, and must therefore be sold cheaply. If you want a potential show winner you should say so: the relationship between buyer and seller has to be an honest one, for there are all kinds of eventualities in future when your breeder may turn out to be a key person.

Puppies that look exceptionally good for showing are often kept for longer, as the breeder needs to see them at 6 months to evaluate them properly. But to begin in showing, you will not need such an illustrious animal.

Study the breed standard ahead of your visit, and perhaps look at one or two of the commentaries published in larger books on the breed. Look at photographs and drawings of champions. Most important of all, go to a show, or a few shows, and talk to people in the know.

When you go for your appointment, it is often best to go alone.

Yorkshire Terrier puppies for sale: all are irresistible

Ask to see as many of the breeder's stock as possible. Some of the pups may have been spoken for before they were born, but check that the whole litter is in good condition, and ask to see both parents if you can.

Judging the puppy

If you are buying for show purposes, a Yorkshire Terrier puppy must be small, with a short back, and its bone should not be too heavy. Never confuse small size with weakness, and the puppy you select should be lively and gay.

Check that the tail has been docked to the right length, and that the dew claws have been expertly removed from the front legs without leaving a scar. The 1980s have seen an upswing in the movement against tail docking and there is a European Convention on Pet Animals that calls for an end to it, though almost all countries that sign it (including Britain, which signed in the autumn of 1987) leave out the clause on tail docking.

However, in response to pressure from vets, the Kennel Club in its 1987 review of breed standards has altered the rules slightly. Instead of simply saying 'docked', the standard now reads 'customarily docked', implying that nothing has changed – yet.

Do not be deterred by the fact that the puppies look black at this time: the colour change begins at 3–4 months, and it will be up to 2–3 years before the mature coat is fixed.

Eyes should be bright and almond-shaped, and not too prominent; a good rule of thumb is to look for a neat, equal-sided triangle made by the nose and the two eyes.

The puppy's back needs to be straight when it stands, neither sagging at the shoulder nor bending upwards in a 'roach back'.

The ears should be triangular and set high up on the head. They will need to be erect when the dog grows up, but are soft and hang down in puppyhood. They should hang forward.

The dew claw is the dog's 'thumb' but serves no functional purpose

dew claw

dew claw removed

dog tick

follicular mite

louse

flea

Fleas, lice and mites are the external parasites of dogs

The teeth should be sharp and white, and should meet in a scissor bite: the front teeth (incisors) close with the upper ones just neatly in front of the lower ones. The large teeth at the corners, of course (the canines) close lower in front of upper.

Each puppy should have a loose, elastic skin. Look under the belly for any redness or rash, and look for signs of parasites (fleas, lice or worms – see page 60).

Listen carefully to what the breeder tells you: most breeders give sound advice on the correct rearing and care of the puppy, and usually on making your choice out of the litter. Make sure it is agreed exactly what the price you pay will buy. Does it include the papers, all signed and handed over on the spot? For every puppy, these should include a diet sheet; and if you are going to show and breed for showing, you must receive (1) the pedigree; and (2) the white-and-green registration document.

Care of the new puppy

Your Yorkie is now spoken for, and it is time to fix a convenient date on which to collect it. Before the day, you should allow yourself time to buy all the necessary equipment and food, and see the vet and arrange for an inspection on or soon after the puppy's first day. The vet may be able to visit your home, and this saves the risk of infection to an uninoculated puppy.

Play pen and bed

The Yorkshire Terrier, when it is old enough for you to take home, is not much larger than a Golden Hamster! Where owners buying puppies of other breeds make their homes safe by respositioning wires and placing objects out of reach, Yorkshire Terrier owners do it the other way round and put the puppy in a pen. Here it cannot be trodden on, fall downstairs or be injured by someone opening a door.

For an indoor playpen, a pair of wire fireguards can be put up facing each other; if the young puppy ever gets the knack of forcing them apart, you will have to tie them together with string.

To let the puppy play outside, construct a small run. This is essentially a rectangular fence of wire mesh and wooden supports, which may be placed on the patio or the lawn.

The next requirement is a bed. A cardboard box – say a shoe box – will do. Take off the lid and cut part of one side down so that the puppy can see the way in. Line the box with newspaper. The puppy will almost certainly start to chew the sides of the box, but this does not matter as it will not be long before it has outgrown this one and can start on a new, larger box.

The first day

Collect your puppy by car if possible. This avoids the risk of picking up diseases from animals met along the way, or germs or parasites on the ground. Bear in mind that this journey is probably the most frightening experience that the animal will undergo in all its life. It is leaving its mother and siblings and being subjected to a range of totally unfamiliar scents, sights and sounds.

Young puppies are very commonly carsick, so remember to lay newspaper on seats and floor, and perhaps place an old towel or blanket on your lap. It is a good idea to collect your puppy in the morning, as this enables the breeder to help by holding back the morning feed. The puppy is less likely to waste it, and is correspondingly more likely to have a good appetite on arrival in your home.

Settling down

Get home as smoothly and quickly as possible, talking soothingly to the puppy, and offer a small feed of cereal and milk on arrival. After feeding, place the puppy on its

The new puppy must be allowed plenty of rest

Having a drink on arrival

toilet area (see page 33) then put it in its box with a soft blanket, and encourage it to sleep. If it whimpers or cries, comfort it and then settle it firmly back in the box.

At this stage the puppy's play periods are about 30 minutes long and are interspersed with long periods of sleep. At night the puppy will probably cry again: offer a well-wrapped stone hot water bottle, or have an infra-red heater suspended over the box for added warmth and comfort.

Plastic baskets are more convenient for cleaning than wicker ones

Puppies and children

Healthy puppies enjoy playing with (kind) children. Teach the children how to groom the puppy; how to carry it correctly, with both arms encompassing the fore and hind legs; how to lift and put down the little dog; and how to help prepare its regular meals.

There are a few basic rules to protect both parties:

- Children must be taught to wash their hands after play sessions with the puppy.
- The puppy needs short sessions of deep sleep after each play session, and children must be taught to respect this. A puppy must never be allowed to become exhausted or overexcited.
- The puppy must not be allowed to play with items small enough for it to swallow or to get stuck in its throat.
- It must not be pulled around on a lead or treated like a toy.

The correct way to carry a puppy

A hard rubber ball is a good toy

More equipment

After a few months you will be able to get a permanent bed for the young dog. The best from many points of view is a plastic one, which is shaped in such a way that it is easy to clean and difficult to chew. If you do not like plastic there are many baskets of different shapes in pet shops, but these will have to be brushed out and cleaned with disinfectant as they have more surfaces that will get dirty.

Yorkshire Terrier puppies will play very happily with small things like yogurt cartons, tea packets or egg boxes. Tissue cartons are just an ideal size for them to clamber in and out of, so you do not need to spend much money on toys. The growing teeth also need rawhide chews on which to bite, or any similar-sized non-toxic item that you can spare.

All dogs need to undergo a vaccination programme

Vaccination programme

Approximate age (take the vet's advice)	**Vaccination**
9 weeks	First canine distemper First canine hepatitis First canine parvovirus } combined First combined leptospirosis
About 12 weeks	Second canine distemper Second canine hepatitis Second canine parvovirus } combined Second combined leptospirosis First rabies (necessary if the dog lives in or will travel to countries where there is rabies; not normally given if dog is not leaving the UK)
14–16 weeks	Second rabies (if applicable)
16–20 weeks	Third canine parvovirus if applicable (depends on circumstances)
Annually	Canine distemper Canine hepatitis Canine parvovirus Leptospirosis } combined booster

Feeding

The breeder is almost certain to give you a diet sheet with the puppy, which tells you exactly what and when to give, as that is what the puppy has been weaned to. It takes a little getting used to, making a 'meal' of not much more than a tablespoon of food!

Each breeder will prescribe a different diet but they will all be within the same general framework: two meals of meat, and two of cereal plus milk. The cereal is very often a baby cereal; and the meat may be chopped rabbit, chicken, lamb or fish, all cooked. Only beef can be served raw.

Child feeding puppy

Here is an excellent diet sheet:

Morning: 1 tablespoon of baby cereal with warm milk. You may add a vitamin supplement. Occasionally substitute scrambled egg.

Midday: $\frac{3}{4}$ tablespoon finely minced cooked meat, mixed with a little fine puppy meal, soaked in gravy; chopped vegetables (about 1 teaspoon); $\frac{1}{4}$ tablet of a nutrient supplement.

Teatime: as morning.

Bedtime: 1 tablespoon of warm milk.

One meal is eliminated by the age of 6 months, the other by 12 months or as early as 8 months if it suits the individual owner and puppy. At the same time, gradually increase all quantities so that while the number of meals is going down, the total quantity fed gradually increases. It is not terribly important which meal becomes the main meal, so you can arrange it to suit your convenience.

Gradually shift the distribution of food as time goes by, enlarging one until the others dwindle to a mere snack, say a saucer of milk or a few biscuits. The main meal will eventually consist of both meat and biscuit (cereal), and the adult dog will eat about 15 g ($\frac{1}{2}$ oz) of meat for every 450 g (1 lb) of its body weight, with a similar total weight of biscuit and milk.

Fresh foods and supplements ensure a healthy, raised diet for the adult dog

Training

Yorkshire Terriers are normally friendly dogs that enjoy training, and they are intelligent, so there is little difficulty in making them understand what they should do. They relate well to their owners and handlers, so that many winners in obedience classes are Yorkies.

House training

This can begin as soon as the puppy of 2 or 3 months has settled in the playpen and got used to its new home. The best method is to designate a special area, normally outside, as the dog's toilet area and try to see that the dog is placed there at all the predictable times when it will need to go.

Improvised playpen for Yorkie pups

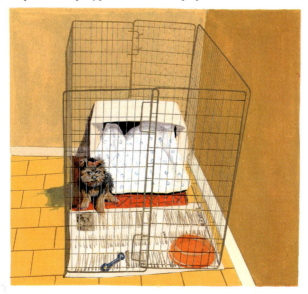

An outdoor run provides a safe play area

These are (**1**) first thing in the morning, and Yorkshire Terriers are usually early risers so you will need to get up smartly to catch them at this time; (**2**) 5–10 minutes after waking from a day-time sleep; (**3**) about 5 minutes after each meal; and (**4**) also put the puppy on its patch last thing at night.

With some puppies, house training proceeds without any hitches, while with others it can seem a never-ending affair. It is one of the most important sets of lessons that a puppy has to learn and it must be given maximum patience.

Whenever the puppy performs in an acceptable manner it must be warmly praised, but do not punish it when it makes a mistake: merely show it that such behaviour is not pleasing.

House manners

When the puppy reaches about 6 months of age and is capable of looking after itself a bit more, you may decide you will allow it the free run of certain areas in the home. It will have a larger territory than its pen and outdoor run, but there will still be areas that are forbidden.

It must learn that these areas are absolutely out of bounds, or for instance that it may go on some furniture but not the armchairs. Once you have decided where it may go, it is absolutely vital to stick to this and never waver from enforcing it. Any time your word of command is ignored with impunity serves to encourage the puppy into further disobedience.

You will find it extremely useful to teach the puppy to go into its bed or basket at a word of command, or even a hand signal. This should never be thought of as a punishment, and can be accompanied with a reward.

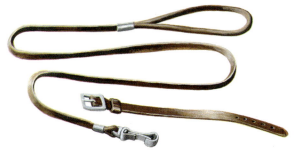

Lead, collar and disc: outside the home, dogs must carry identification

The collar and lead

The Yorkie at the age of 10 weeks has such a small neck that a ladies' watch strap serves as an effective collar. Alternatively, there are purpose-made ones. For the first week of lead training, clip on a very light lead to the puppy's collar and leave it to trail on the ground for short periods.

Follow this with some more serious training: hold the lead and encourage the puppy to walk with you, on your left.

Never use the led as a means of pulling the puppy along, nor to smack it. Praise the puppy whenever it walks freely forward. The lead will become an object of pleasure to the dog, never an instrument of punishment.

Yorkies love a good training session

Basic obedience training

The very best way to learn to train your dog is to enrol in a dog-training class. These cater for all standards from the basics to competitive obedience work and besides giving you thousands of ideas, they provide a chance for the dog to socialize too.

Preliminary classes cover the basic commands, walking at heel and coming to call, while those who wish to progress to showing may attend ringcraft lessons.

Basic training is essentially about teaching your puppy to be considerate and obedient, to come *immediately* when called and to have acceptable manners in the home. Play is an important aspect in teaching manners, and it is vital that your dog really loves and respects you, so that you become its 'pack leader'.

Serious training should begin when your puppy reaches 6–8 months. You will be able to graduate to ringcraft and formal obedience work whenever you are ready and have the time.

General care

Eyes

Yorkshire Terriers occasionally get a mild eye infection: the eyes become inflamed and give off a discharge. Cure this by bathing in a mild saline solution, or you can use the medications sold in chemists' shops for human eyes. Dip a cotton wool swab in the solution and wipe from the outer corner to the inner one. Then discard the swab and repeat with a fresh one. Treat each eye separately and never use the same swab on both eyes.

Ears

Look at the ears each week to check for a build-up of wax. Dry swabs will lift this out, together with any dirt, but you can use damp swabs for more resistant grime as long as you make sure no water trickles down into the ear.

A heavy-build-up of greasy-looking discharge inside the ear flaps is probably a sign of ear mites (*Odectes* mites – see page 61).

If your dog constantly shakes its head it may have a grass awn (seed with its long spike) stuck down the ear and this might need the vet's help to get it out.

Teeth

The first teeth start to appear when the puppy is 3 weeks old and are generally all grown by 6 weeks. These are the milk teeth – they fall out from about 12 weeks to 16 weeks, when the permanent teeth grow. This period when new teeth are 'erupting' beneath and between the milk teeth is one when special care is needed, as teeth will be crowded in the mouth and food particles can very easily get trapped for a long time, leading to dental disease and even tooth loss.

Clean the dog's teeth at regular intervals. The best

method for the Yorkie is to use a small tooth brush with water, salt water or else toothpaste.

If tartar (a hard deposit) appears on the teeth, despite a good diet with hard biscuit, the vet will scale it.

Nails and paws

Your dog has four black nails (claws) on each foot (dew claws are higher up but will have been removed). Unless the dog does quite a lot of running on roads and pavements the claws will get too long and you will need to trim them. Many of the 'guillotine-type' pair of claw clippers are too large for toy dogs' nails, but they come in various sizes, so you will find the smallest about right.

Sometimes the paws suffer from cysts between the toes, which are small swellings that will make the dog hobble or limp. These can be cured quite quickly by a visit to your local vet.

Claw clipping is painless if you avoid the quick

the quick
untrimmed claw

claw trimmed to
avoid sensitive quick

Essential grooming aids

Trimming the coat

Buy a small pair of scissors with round ends or if possible the half-disc ends for the delicate work of trimming the fur from the ears. The hair is cut from the top half of the ear flap, to lighten the tip so that it will stand up well, and to enhance the natural shape.

Use these scissors to cut some of the excess fur from round the pads of the feet, too, as these can get in the way and are a nuisance when wet.

Grooming

It is really part of the puppy's training to get used to being handled and groomed, and so all the same principles apply: the dog should enjoy the whole performance. Talk to the puppy and give praise at every opportunity, and never scold; merely indicate that bad behaviour is not approved.

When your Yorkie is a puppy its fur is short and fine, so it will be a simple matter to groom. Go through the motions of grooming an adult dog, so it is an established routine from the start.

Wear an apron and place the puppy on its back on your lap, where it will be an easy matter to brush the inner thighs, chest and front legs. Then stand it on its feet and brush the whole coat first up towards the spine, then down from the spine towards the ground, leaving a neat parting along the spine.

When the puppy grows up and develops a long coat you will need to keep dipping the brush and comb in pure water – not tap water with its minerals and chemicals, but either distilled or rain water. The tips of the hair are brittle and may break off or split unless softened in this way.

How to put the coat in 'crackers'

A jacket protects the 'crackered' coat

A show dog's coat is protected from hair breakage by applying oil: this does not take long and you can choose an oil most suited to your dog: this may be lanolin and coconut oil, almond oil, baby oil or any well-chosen hairdressing oil.

The greatest pride of the owner of a show dog is in the 'crackering' of the coat, which is done as soon as the coat begins to grow long and reaches to the ground. Its purpose is to protect the long, delicate coat from breakage caused by scratching, rubbing or by being tugged at by other dogs.

A cracker is made by folding a bundle of hairs, from an area of about 5×5 cm (2×2 in) of the dog's coat, inside a rectangle of tissue paper or fine material (many owners use nappy liners). The wrapping is placed under the bundle of hairs and each side is folded in. The wrapped-up bundle of hair is then folded in half, and then in half again, so it looks a bit like the kind of firecracker that used to be seen on Guy Fawkes' night.

Finally groomed and ready for the ring

A show dog normally has 21 crackers, and wears a cotton jacket to cover them, giving protection and stopping the hair oil from getting on your clothing or furniture. The dog will also have to have small socks (usually only on the hind feet) to prevent it from scratching at the crackers or the delicate coat.

Tying the top knot

Bathing

Pet dogs can be given a bath as required, which may be fortnightly or even monthly; if they are kept close-trimmed, it could be considerably less often. Show dogs, with their oiled coat, will certainly have a bath before going to the show, and perhaps once a week at other times.

Both will need shampoo and hair conditioner, but with a show dog you will need to apply shampoo twice, with extra rinsings as necessary.

The puppies are so small that great emphasis is placed on bathing with maximum speed, to get the puppy clean and dried again before there is any chance of a chill. You can experiment with ways of lining up bowls of warm water so that you can dip the puppy in them in succession for a quick wash and rinse.

Fully grown dogs with long coats must be thoroughly dried after their bath, for if you tie up a damp coat, it will be wavy when it comes out of the crackers. Don't forget to groom a dressing of oil into the dry coat – unless this is a show day.

Breeding

Breeding is the most fascinating part of keeping dogs and if your bitch is even-tempered and grows to a suitable size you may decide to let her have a litter in her second year. The best age is around 18 months, and four or five litters are considered the maximum for her lifetime in the interests of her health and well-being.

You will have to afford the time and expense, but if you make the right choice of stud and manage the bitch and litter properly it is reasonable to hope for a return from the sale of the puppies that might at least repay your investment. Your outlay will be mainly in the stud fee, the veterinary bill, the cost of special feeding and the cost of inoculations.

The question of size

The Yorkshire Terrier is a toy breed and is the product of selective breeding to achieve small size. Many litters, especially in past years, included large puppies but the main interest has always been in the smaller ones.

The result is that the breed still has it in its genes to produce puppies that will not be conveniently sized for their mother to give birth. Responsible breeders will use a bitch of, say, 2.6–2.8 kg (5½–6 lb), mating her to a dog of only 1.8 kg (4 lb) or less.

It is irresponsible to use an oversize bitch with a really tiny sire, as some of the progeny are likely to have difficulties in giving birth. Apart from this, puppies from a large-built mother will probably have rather coarse lines and will not be good for showing.

If you are thinking of breeding from a small bitch, have her examined by a vet; in fact you would not be doing wrong to have any Yorkie bitch examined before making further plans. Find out if her pelvic bones are the right size and that all is in order before you proceed.

Choosing a mate

The usual strategy for breeding show dogs is line breeding, in which matings are arranged between animals that share a few of their relatives and come from similar broad family backgrounds. Line breeding helps to produce animals that concentrate the genes for their family characteristics; it can often produce dogs with a remarkable ability to impose their distinctive 'stamp' on future generations.

Take the advice of the breeder from whom you obtained your bitch, who will most likely be able to put you in touch with a stud within the correct line. You will be advised to find a stud who is complementary to your bitch – one whose good features match up with the weaker points in your bitch – with a view to improving the line.

Mother with pups in an informal whelping box

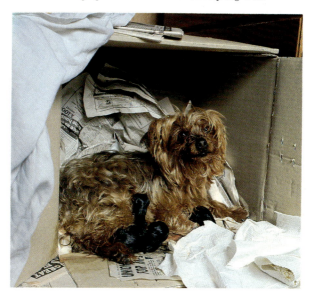

The oestrous cycle

The bitch has a sexually receptive phase twice a year known as the 'oestrous' period or 'season'. At this time she will mate and conceive puppies. Most bitches come into season for the first time at 9–12 months of age, and oestrus (spelt without the second 'o' when used as a noun) recurs at intervals of 6–9 months, until late in life.

The signs of oestrus are usually clear. The bitch may become irritable or extra sensitive, and may also become extra affectionate. The vulva will enlarge and become puffy; and a bloodstained discharge appears (this is known as 'showing colour'). The bitch will frequently lick the genital area.

The chief sign that she is ready for mating is that the red discharge ceases and a straw-coloured fluid appears. This is normally between the 10th and 18th day, but early and late cases do occur.

Going to stud

See that the bitch is at the peak of health and in perfect condition, free from parasites and up to date with the year's booster injections. Get in touch with the stud owner when the bitch comes into season, so that he (or she) is forewarned that the day will soon come; and make a provisional appointment.

Yorkshire Terriers are very delicate and both owners will need to be present at the mating to handle the dogs and see that accidents do not happen. Any violent movement or struggling on either part may hurt or harm the sexual organs, or cause a fall which might lead to injury.

The anatomy of the dog is such that the mated pair are unable to separate immediately after mating. The dog will wish to get down from the mounted position, and it may be better for his owner to help by lifting him down; but the two will remain connected, back to back, in an attitude known as the tie.

The tie may last from a few minutes to an hour and the

pair may even fall asleep, to wake up separated. If a tie does not occur, conception is still likely.

One mating is usually sufficient, but you should make sure in advance that it is agreed between you and the stud owner whether or not a second service (usually within 48 hours) is included in the price.

Pay the stud fee and see that you get a certificate recording the mating and the pedigree of the stud. Keep this, as you will need it later for registering the puppies.

The puppies will be born 63 days from the day of the first mating, if all goes normally; but exceptions are common and whelping can be up to a week late or early without any need to take special veterinary measures.

Pregnancy

For a month, there will be no obvious sign of pregnancy. Then, in week 5, the bitch may appear quieter and more affectionate. She may be less inclined to romp or run fast when she goes out for exercise – though some mothers are as irrepressible as ever.

By week 6 her abdomen will have enlarged notice-ably, and her teats will have swollen. She may need to urinate more frequently now, and she may become intolerant of other dogs.

Week 9 is the last week, and her abdomen will be very distended. There will probably be milk in her teats. Her vulva will look soft and enlarged. She may be very affectionate. It may be difficult for her to get into a comfortable resting position.

Her food intake should be increased from week 5 by adding an extra meal, with a vitamin and mineral supplement. In week 6, increase the quantity of food in the additional meal slightly, and restrict the more strenuous parts of her exercise.

During weeks 7 and 8 her food will be divided into three well-spaced meals, giving a total volume of about 1½ times normal. Give food of the best quality, and allow her to drink a little milk in addition to her normal fresh water. Do not overdo the mineral and vitamin supplements, but ensure that any nutrient deficiency is balanced.

Continue with periods of exercise, but these will be rather limited, without strenuous running or jumping. In week 9, treat her with all consideration; feed her a little and often, allow her to exercise as she pleases and ensure that she is able to relieve herself as often as she wishes.

Give her a whelping box, and encourage her to examine and explore it to her heart's content, so that she will take to it in place of her normal bed. The whelping box is commonly of the type with a hinged lid as well as a door at the front: this is because many owners prefer to have the box on a table for easy viewing, and an open-sided box would not be safe. The bitch is lifted out and back into the box, and the front door kept closed, so there is no risk of a fall.

You must be able to heat the room where whelping is to take place if the need arises. Either heat the whole

Whelping box with a heating lamp

Unborn puppies inside the uterus

room or hang a heat lamp over the whelping box.
Newborn puppies can sometimes become separated
from their mother, lose body heat and then develop
hypothermia and die, unless there is supplementary
heating.

Essential equipment

- Lots of clean newspaper for bedding.
- A bowl of water, soap and a towel for hand washing.
- A pair of sterilized stainless steel scissors.
- Some clean towels for drying the puppies.
- Plastic sack for soiled bedding and towels.
- A large box with a hot water bottle and blanket, in
  which to keep the puppies if their mother cannot
  cope with them.
- Scales, notebook and pencil for recording each
  birth.

Normal delivery
Puppy emerges,
forepaws and nose first

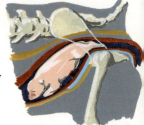

Posterior delivery
Hind feet first

Modes of presentation for birth

Labour

A common sign of the first stage of labour, in which the
cervix relaxes and dilates, and the puppies rotate ready
for birth, is the bitch's refusal of her food. She may
become very restless and look anxious, and she may
pant frequently.

The second stage of labour begins with the bitch
straining, and by now she is almost certain to be lying in
the whelping box. She may grunt or cry out, and once
again pant. If it is her first litter she may appear
frightened and walk in circles, but she should be kept as
calm as possible and given privacy.

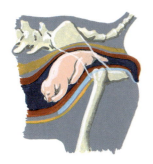

Breech delivery
Tail and rump first

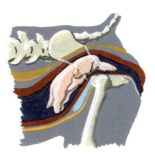

Head presented laterally
The most likely
mode to cause difficulties.
Often needs manipulation
for safe birth.

The straining produces the first water bag: this looks like a black or grey balloon, and she usually ruptures it by biting or licking; this releases a gush of greenish-grey amniotic fluid. The first puppy should follow quickly, born encased in a membrane which the bitch licks away.

Her licking stimulates the puppy's first breath. If she neglects this duty, you must remove the membrane, otherwise the puppy will suffocate the moment the oxygen supply from the placenta is cut off. Clear the puppy's mouth and nostrils of mucus to allow a clear passage of air.

*Reviving a lifeless pup by draining
its blocked breathing passage*

The third stage of labour is the expulsion of the placenta, and usually occurs about 15 minutes after the birth of the puppy. The bitch eats the placenta and bites through the umbilical cord. She then cleans up the birth fluids, licks the puppy and her own vulva, and settles down before the next puppy presents itself for birth.

Yorkshire Terrier litters average about 3–5 in number, though they commonly vary between 1 and 7. The puppies may be born at regular intervals or they may come in batches or pairs with long intervals of rest ($\frac{1}{2}$–2 hours) in between.

It is better to leave the bitch alone during whelping, assisting her only if she neglects her duties, or if the puppies come so quickly that she cannot attend to them all. The owner's role should be passive, observant and comforting, but ready to call the vet if necessary.

When the litter is born, provide her with a drink of warm milk and praise her for her splendid work. Shut the whelping box lid down and leave her with a little light reaching her through the front door so that she can see her brood. Arrange a visit from the vet as soon as is convenient, but otherwise you should be her only visitor.

If things go wrong

Breeding is normally straightforward from start to finish, but there are occasional mishaps and it is impossible to predict when and to which bitch they will happen, so it is really advisable to keep in touch with the vet from the start. The telephone number of the surgery should be pinned up next to the telephone, and you should give advance warning during office hours as soon as you feel labour is likely to start.

Puppies may appear lifeless, when all you need do is to hold them upside down to drain the fluid; or a young or inexperienced bitch may seem afraid of her first puppy and not want to suckle it, in which case the box you have ready with the hot water bottle will come in useful until, with luck, she decides to accept the puppy after all.

Toy dogs have a higher frequency of Caesarian births than other breeds (see page 44), so remember that this is always a possibility. Whatever happens, if the bitch has strained for an hour and no puppy appears, or if the puppy is part of the way out and the bitch cannot complete expulsion, call the vet.

You may also find yourself facing the awful situation of the loss of the bitch; if this happens, or even if she is ill or simply has not enough milk for her litter, you may have to take on the task of hand rearing the puppies.

Hand rearing is a long and arduous undertaking and it is not always successful, though it is always an exhilaration to have found your way through this trying time and rescued the tiny puppies. But get every bit of advice you can from the vet or from an experienced breeder. There are special foods and purpose-made feeding equipment for supplying the little pups with the tiny quantities of food they need.

Caring for the puppies

During the first 10 days, puppies have their eyes tightly closed and they do little but feed, eliminate and sleep. At 3 days the vet will dock the tails and remove the dew claws (these are placed like 'thumbs' and appear as an extra claw on the front legs, sometimes the hind legs too). This should be done well out of the mother's sight.

It is as well to clip the ordinary claws a little, to prevent puppies with long claws from damaging the bitch's teats as they scrabble for milk.

Check the navels daily and report any sign of inflammation or swelling. The dried cords will have dropped off after 2 or 3 days.

Although their hearing is not very developed at this stage, you should talk to the puppies at all times to accustom them to the human voice.

Once their eyes are open, the puppies begin to exhibit the first play behaviour, and they start to lift their bodies up on to their legs rather than squirming around in the whelping box. The first teeth come at 5 weeks and are needle-sharp.

At 20 days the puppies can see and hear and are well up on their feet. At this stage, socialization should begin and they will take a positive interest in their brothers and sisters.

Handle the pups gently and firmly, to get them used to you and to having all parts of their bodies examined: ears, teeth, coat, paws and underbelly. Give them their first dose of worming medicine at 3 weeks, and a second dose at 5 weeks.

To cater for the bitch's needs in lactation, feed her about double quantities in the first week, gradually increasing to at least treble in the fifth. She should be fed to appetite at least three times a day, and should have a good quality diet with added vitamins and minerals as advised by the vet.

The puppies should accept their first 'solid' food – baby cereal with a little honey for example – at 3 weeks, and their demands on the bitch will lessen about the fifth week. At 4–5 weeks they will eat as many as four meals a day. Weaning should be complete by 6–7 weeks.

By 6 weeks they are walking firmly, playing and defecating without their mother's stimulation. The baby teeth are firmly established and they use them in mock fighting and to exercise their jaws on a chew or small bone such as a rib.

Their mother's enthusiasm will have gradually diminished from its initial maternal concern, and now she will want to spend only the briefest periods with her offspring. You should place them in a play pen, at first only for short periods, providing a few safe toys. Give water in good solid drinking bowls.

The weanling puppy

The period in a puppy's life between weaning and settling into its new home can be critical. It is a period of rapid development, both physical and mental.

Puppies are usually sold at about 8 weeks of age and it is important that the fortnightly doses of worming medicine are given. These should have begun at 3 weeks and continued at 5, 7, 9, 11 and 13 weeks. Thereafter the puppy must be wormed at 6-month intervals.

The period of socialization is the period from weaning to about 14 weeks. It is during this time that the young dog learns to respond socially and to recognize its own species. Ideally, puppies should be taken from their mother and siblings at about 8–10 weeks, having enjoyed the first part of the period of socialization with dogs, while having the remainder in which to explore and develop lasting relationships with humans.

History of the breed

The Yorkshire Terrier was bred in Victorian England in answer to a fashionable demand for a miniature version of the lively terriers that were commonly found in Yorkshire. Terriers are active, alert dogs that excel in hunting small animals, often underground. In the countryside their quarry is the fox or the rabbit; since industrial times began, terriers have been the companion of the working man. In Victorian Yorkshire, after a week's toil in the mill or mine, vermin hunting was a traditional way of relaxing.

The breeders drew on a number of dogs, mainly Scottish ones. These had been brought by Scottish weavers who had migrated to Yorkshire in the middle of the 19th century: their dogs were Paisley Terriers (also called Clydesdale Terriers) and Waterside Terriers. The Waterside had a longish coat that was bluish grey in colour, and it was a fairly small dog, weighing between 2.5 kg (6 lb) and 9 kg (20 lb). This made the Waterside a good start for miniaturization, and the breeders drew on its stock extensively as they worked over the decades to the Yorkshire Terrier size.

The Clydesdale was another small breed, rarely exceeding 8 kg (18 lb). Its descendant the Skye Terrier was used to give length and silkiness to the coat of the miniature. Another Scottish breed, the Dandie Dinmont Terrier, may have helped as well.

Other breeds used were the Maltese (also for silkiness) and the old rough-coated Black and Tan Terrier from England, which was important for contributing its colours and pattern. The Yorkie's blue colouring came partly from a blue-and-tan version of this dog, and partly from the Waterside.

As the Yorkshire Terrier began very much as a weaver's dog, there were jokes about the natural enthusiasm of its owners for a dog with a long, silky coat. Yorkshire Terriers attained astonishing lengths of coat; for example, there was one dog in 1900 that weighed 2.5 kg (5½ lb), and had a coat 60 cm (24 in) long all round.

The famous Yorkshire Terrier Huddersfield Ben, born in 1865, was an extremely well-proportioned, sprightly little dog who was a first-class ratter. Apart from having a brilliant show career himself he bred very true, imposing his qualities on his innumerable progeny, so that many of the best specimens we have today are related to him.

Another early contributor to the present-day stock was Mrs M A Foster's Champion Ted, who won 265 prizes. Mrs Foster bought him at Heckmondwicke Show in Yorkshire in 1887, when he was 4. His weight was 2 kg (4½ lb), his height at shoulder 22 cm (9 in) and his length from his nose to the set-on of his tail was 43 cm (17 in). The length of his coat across the shoulders was 46 cm (18 in).

Known for four centuries, the Skye Terrier is an ancestor of today's Yorkie

The now extinct Clydesdale Terrier, another ancestor of the present-day Yorkie

The breed began to attract the interest of the middle classes and consequently efforts were redoubled in multiplying the breed for profit. Gradually the Yorkshire Terrier came to be a fashionable miniature, at a weight of between 1.4 kg (3 lb) and 3.2 kg (7 lb).

The name Yorkshire Terrier was introduced in 1874, when the Kennel Club entered it in its stud book as the 'Broken-haired Scotch Terrier or Yorkshire Terrier' (broken-haired referred to the fact that the coat was not of one whole colour). For some years dogs from the same litter competed in the Yorkshire Terrier class or as Scotch Terriers proper, depending on which class suited their size.

As owners often kept larger bitches for breeding, using very small males as studs, litters often contained puppies that grew to a wide range of different sizes, so that there has always been a plentiful supply of oversize specimens that will fetch no price as show dogs, and are available cheaply as pets.

Basic health care

Provided you keep a constant watch on hygiene and correct diet, and are continually aware of the need to avoid contact with poisons such as warfarin, metaldehyde, paraquat and any household supplies of solvents or acid, basic health care is reduced to manageable proportions. Preventive measures include regular checks and the routine worming doses and inoculations.

In cases of illness the vet will play a key role, for there are many cases when it will be plain for all to see that the dog is ill, but without the vet to diagnose the illness you simply do not know where to start. But here are a few of the commonest ailments, some of which you will be able to treat without outside help.

Ear disease: Head shaking, scratching at the ears or the onset of an unpleasant smell may indicate a disease of the dog's ears. Healthy ears should be shiny inside with pale skin, free from dirt, wax or debris. Ear diseases must be treated without delay, to avoid excessive scratching, and to save the dog from the depression that may come with the constant pain.

Ear mites are described under *Mites*. Other diseases of the ear may be treated with antibiotic or anti-inflammatory drugs, plus an ointment or lotion.

Eye ailments: Conjunctivitis is an inflammation of the lining of the eye; it is generally treated by bathing the eyes in a saline solution and applying antibiotic drops or ointment.

A foreign body may get lodged in the eye. One eye partially closed or watering may indicate the presence of a foreign body such as a grass seed. Once this has been identified it may be removed with the corner of a paper tissue, or by flushing the eye with a syringe of warmed saline solution. However, if there seems to be an object but you cannot see it, you will need help from the vet.

Blue-looking eyes (blue cornea) may simply be the after-effect of an infection, or of certain types of vaccination, but it might be caused by the formation of a cataract, which cannot be prevented and is difficult to cure.

Corneal ulcers can form and are so painful that the dog constantly rubs at the affected eye. The eye may be partially closed, with the third eyelid visible. Eye ointment can cure an ulcer, but persistent ones may require surgery.

Fleas: These small wingless insects suck the dog's blood, causing irritation and sometimes an allergic skin reaction. A heavy infestation has a debilitating effect on the dog due to blood loss and lack of proper rest; but worse still, any infestation at all can give the dog tapeworm, whose tiny eggs can be carried in the flea.

Special soaps, shampoos and sprays may be used to rid the dog of adult fleas in its coat, and the treatment should be extended to the dog's bedding and exercise areas to eradicate eggs and larvae (see page 24).

Lice: Another type of wingless insect that lives and breeds on the dog. Lice use specially adapted mouthparts to pierce the skin and suck the animal's blood and tissue fluids. You can eradicate the adult insects fairly easily with an insecticide, but they leave their eggs cemented tightly to the dog's hair and the only way to destroy these is to continue spraying with insecticide at weekly intervals until there are none left.

Mites: More closely related to spiders than insects, these little creatures can cause intense irritation and depression. All species of mite are difficult to eradicate and you will in fact need to go to the vet for a prescription. Treatment must be kept up for a long time.

Follicular mange mites attack the hair follicles, and in puppies patches of hair fall out around the head, eyes, muzzle and paws, while in older dogs the hair loss is more generalized.

Ear mites (*Odectes* mites) live in the ear canal. They can be particularly maddening for the dog.

Ringworm: This is not a worm but a fungus that parasitizes the dog's skin. Dogs with ringworm generally have skin lesions (damaged places) that appear as roughly circular, scaly patches, where the hair has broken off leaving stubby ends. There may also be crusty scabs and pustules.

The vet will take a skin sample for laboratory analysis to confirm ringworm. Treatment is a combination of systemic drugs and skin dressings. Ringworm is contagious and transmissible to man, and any dog with ringworm must be isolated until pronounced cured.

Worms: Even the best-bred dogs can suffer from internal parasites, which are known to us as worms. The first worming dose is given at 5 weeks, then at fortnightly intervals until 13 weeks, longer if necessary.

Tapeworms belong to two types: *Dipylidium* tapeworms which are carried by fleas, and *Taenia* tapeworms which infect the meat of cattle, sheep and rabbits. If the dog swallows a flea, or eats part of a carcass found in the countryside, it can be infected. The first sign of this may be when small segments of the worm, looking like live grains of rice, are seen around the dog's anus or in its bedding. Tapeworms are eradicated by dosing with a specific vermifuge.

Roundworms are very common in young puppies and are dangerous as they can cause serious illness in children. The puppy may have a pot-bellied appearance, and will suffer from bouts of diarrhoea.

Index

Figures in italics refer to illustrations